Siblings
You're Stuck with Each Other,
So Stick Together

Siblings

You're Stuck with Each Other, So Stick Together

by James J. Crist, Ph.D.,
& Elizabeth Verdick

Illustrated by Steve Mark

free spirit
PUBLISHING®

Library of Congress Cataloging-in-Publication Data
Crist, James J.
    Siblings : you're stuck with each other, so stick together / by James J. Crist and Elizabeth Verdick ; illustrated by Steve Mark.
        p. cm.—(Laugh & learn series)
    Includes index.
    ISBN 978-1-57542-336-4
1. Brothers and sisters—Juvenile literature. 2. Family—Juvenile literature. I. Verdick, Elizabeth. II. Mark, Steve. III. Title.
    BF723.S43C75 2010
    306.875—dc22

                  2009025453

ISBN: 978-1-57542-336-4

The quotations on page 53 are copyright © 2001 and 2002 by the Associated Press.

Reading Level Grade 4; Interest Level Ages 8–13;
Fountas & Pinnell Guided Reading Level Q

Edited by Eric Braun
Designed by Tasha Kenyon

15 14 13 12 11 10 9
Printed in Hong Kong
P17201218

Free Spirit Publishing Inc.
6325 Sandburg Road, Suite 100
Minneapolis, MN 55427-3674
(612) 338-2068
help4kids@freespirit.com
www.freespirit.com

Dedication

To the young people who have shared their stories
of their siblings with me and allowed me to help
them, and hopefully to help other kids as well. To my
siblings—I love all of you more than words can say.
—JC

To Olivia and Zach, for everything you teach each
other and everything you've taught me. And to my
sisters, Suzanne and Erica, and my brother Mark,
the best siblings ever.
—EV

Contents

A Message for Y-O-U

Hey, you.
You there.

Yeah, that's right,
You.
The one reading.

This book is about sisters, brothers, and getting along. Every sibling relationship has ups and downs, twists and turns, and moments of AAAACK! (Kind of like a roller coaster.) But you can smooth out the ride and have more fun. We wrote this book to help you do it.

It would be really cool if your siblings read the book, too, but that might not happen. Maybe they can't even read yet. Or maybe you'll put this book right where they can find it—*hint hint*—and it still won't get read. That's okay because we have a message especially for *you*.

You live in a family, and your family is your training ground for learning to get along with other people in life. Getting along is challenging no matter how awesome you or your family may be. You'll need practice and some patience, too.

Every idea in this book starts with you. That's because getting along with others really comes down to being the best **YOU** you can be. (Corny but true.) There are probably at least a *few* things you would like to change about your relationship with your siblings. Well, the one person you can change in this world is yourself. The new ways *you* decide to act and speak may inspire your sisters or brothers, or the rest of your family, to follow your lead.

So give yourself a pat on the back, or take a little bow—you deserve some credit for what you're about to do.

Quick Quiz

A *sibling* is:

1. a kid who wears a lot of "bling"

2. that pest who bugs you day and night

3. a brother or sister

4. another word for "attention hog" (oink, oink)

5. someone who's there for you in good times and bad times—maybe for a lifetime

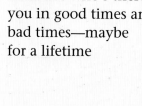

Answer: 3 for sure, and 5 we hope.

But if your brother wears a lot of bling or your sister steals the spotlight every chance she gets, you might have answered 1 or 4 *and* 2, and you'd be right.

Whether your sibling is flashy, annoying, or just plain weird, he or she is part of your family. *Families are forever.* That means you've got a bond—and you've gotta bond. This book will show you how.

Can You Relate?

Being siblings means you and your brother or sister share one parent or two. But families come in all shapes and sizes—they're never one-size-fits-all. Each family fits together in its own way, like a one-of-a-kind jigsaw puzzle. You might have . . .

Siblings by birth

So, you and your sister or brother have the same mom and dad.

Half-siblings

The term "half-sibling" means you and your sib* share only one birth parent. You might have the same mom but different dads, or the same dad but different moms.

*Sib is short for *sibling*. But way more fun to say (and read).

Stepsiblings

You may get "stepsibs" if one of your parents marries someone else. Your new parent becomes your stepparent, and that stepparent's kids become your stepsibs. Even if you feel like stepping on your stepsibs sometimes, learning to get along with them can make life less stressful and more fun.

Adopted siblings

An adopted child may be of any age or race but when she or he becomes part of your family, you become siblings. Even if you're not related by birth or by your parents' marriage, you're now family.

Some parents temporarily take care of a child in need of a stable home. This is called *fostering*. (So you might have a foster sibling for a while.) If the foster parents decide to adopt, the child can become part of the family forever.

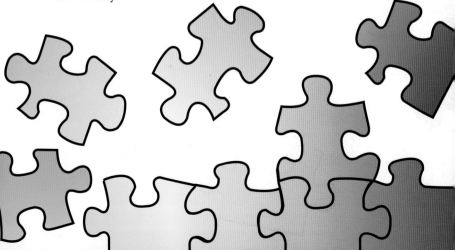

Your family may be big or small—there's no "right" way for a family to look or be. The important thing to know is that you and your siblings are linked by more than just your parent(s).

- **You have many of the same experiences and memories.**

- **You probably share the same home, at least some of the time.**

- **You're connected by . . . love. (Wait! Don't gag! The love is there, or at least it can be.)**

Strange *but* TRUE

The relationship you have with a sister or brother may be the **l-o-n-g-e-s-t** relationship you ever have in your life. Think about it. You not only grow up together but you may also grow *old* together.

When you're grown up, you can hang out, celebrate holidays with each other, or even travel together. If you and your sibs have kids someday, they'll all be cousins—and may become friends for life, too.

What are sibs good for?

If you didn't have a brother or sister, life sure would be different—but not necessarily better. That's because a sib can be:

your friend

your buddy

your ally (someone who's on your side)

your helper

your secret-sharer

your protector

your mentor (someone who guides you)

your role model!

7 super things about sibs

1. Sibs are there for you.

When you want to play, hang out, joke around, talk, or just be next to someone, you don't have to pick up the phone—you have someone right at home. Your sibs are with you early in the morning or late at night, times when it's not as convenient to be around friends. And your sibs are often there for you during life's weirder moments, like when Aunt Bertie tells you long, boring stories about her cats. Best of all, your sibs are there to share the fun times—school breaks, birthdays, holidays, and special family celebrations.

2. Sibs can help you.

Need advice? Help with chores or homework? Got a problem you just can't solve on your own? Ask your sister or brother. A sib can be a great resource for you, especially if you're willing to help out in return. Older sibs often have good advice because they've been there. Younger sibs can be good listeners or "cheerer-uppers."

3. Sibs know the real you.

Even your closest friends don't always see every side of you. They may not know what you're like the moment you wake up, or on a bad day, or when you're crying your eyes out over a really sad movie. But your sibs know—because with them, you're totally yourself (and they love you anyway).

4. Sibs can share stuff with you.

A great thing about having sibs is that you can share games, electronics, sports equipment, and books. If you have older (or larger) sibs, they can hand down their clothes. If you have younger sibs, you get the fun of playing with toys you may have outgrown or doing activities usually meant for younger kids (finger paint all you want, no questions asked). Here are some other things you can share: secrets, dreams, hopes, and fears.

5. There's more "brain power."

Sometimes, you may need help with homework or a school project. Other times, you might need some pointers while working on an athletic skill. Maybe you're having trouble reaching a goal or solving a problem. If you and a sib work on these things together, you have twice the brain power than you have when working alone. It can be fun to help each other out.

6. There's room to grow.

The relationships you have with your siblings help teach you about yourself and the world. You learn about handling strong emotions like anger and disappointment. You see how your words affect the people close to you. And you discover that everyone needs a little something called *unconditional love*. (It means people love you for who you are, through and through, no matter what you do.)

7. Sibs look out for each other— and up to each other.

Maybe your brother watches out for you on the playground. Maybe your sister is your role model, inspiring you to work on your goals. Maybe your siblings teach you new skills—or you teach them. One of the coolest things about having siblings is that you know they have your back (and you have theirs). That can really boost your confidence.

May I Take your Order?

True or false: Before you were born, you and your sibs played rock-paper-scissors to decide who got to be born first.

Answer: True!

Nah, it's false. Nobody gets to choose when they're born. But the birth order in your family can play an important role in how you see yourself, your parents, your sibs, and the world.

> He's the **oldest**—he does everything the best.

> My **little bro** is always copying me—make him stop!

Have you ever noticed how birth order—oldest, middle, youngest—plays a part in how you get along (or don't get along) with your sibs? Read on for an insider's look at birth order. See if some of what you learn is true for you and your family. But remember, no birth order position is better than any other—they're just different and each one has its ups and downs.

> I'm the **middle** kid—no one notices me.

> But she'll always be **older** and get to do everything first!

> How come my **older** brother gets to stay up later? No fair!

> She's the **baby**—everybody spoils her.

Note: If you have lots of siblings or you and your sibs are far apart in age, some of the birth order information might not be true for you. Being the only boy or the only girl in a group of siblings can make a difference, too.

Oldest sibs

> **❝** Being the oldest is both good and bad. The good part is you get to stay up later and have more privileges. The bad part is that you get used to having your parents all to yourself until your sister or brother is born—then you have to share. **❞**
> *Boy, age 10*✳

The oldest sibling is the first child born to his or her parents. With no other kids around, oldest sibs get all of their parents' time and attention. And everything the oldest child does—first steps, first day of kindergarten, losing the first tooth—is a BIG deal to the parents because it's new. Firstborns often feel special because they don't have to share their parents (until the next baby comes along). Firstborns are also "take-charge" kinds of people—maybe because they're used to impressing their parents or being responsible for younger sibs.

✳Quotes that appear in an orange bubble are the real words of real kids the authors have talked to.

Many oldest children:

☑ Want to do things "perfectly"

☑ Are high achievers

☑ Like to be leaders

☑ Want to please others

☑ Tend to take care of others

☑ Are more serious and responsible

When a second child is born, the first child may not be too thrilled. After all, the parents are busier and have more responsibilities, and it's harder to get their attention. Even though parents say they have enough love for two children (or more), kids don't always believe it. That's when the jealousy monster knocks on the door. (For more on jealousy, see pages 49–54 . . . and lock that door!)

Middle children

> **"** When you're in the middle, you're kind of in between. I don't get the privileges of my older brother, and I'm not babied like my little sister. I sometimes feel left out, but I can also do my own thing—like when it's just two of us siblings around, I can play the youngest OR the oldest. **"**
>
> *Boy, age 11*

Being a middle child can be tough. You may not get to do as many cool things as older sibs, and you probably don't get the amount of attention that the youngest child does. So, it may be harder to feel special. Do you ever feel like you're fighting to get noticed?

What you're like as a middle child may depend on how you view your older siblings. If you see them as stronger and smarter, you might think you can't compete, so you find ways to stand on your own and be different. Or, if you're jealous of your older sibs, you may try to annoy them just to make their life difficult. On the other hand, if you have a good relationship with your older sibs, you might try to be more like them.

Middle siblings often:

☑ Try to help others work out conflicts

☑ Are independent

☑ Are more relaxed and easygoing

☑ Act friendly and get along well with peers

☑ Aren't as eager to please other people

☑ May be less motivated to succeed in school

Being a middle child has a cool perk: You get lots of chances to learn how to get along with people older and younger than you are.

The youngest

> 66 I'm the youngest of three girls. Sometimes I feel left out. They're older so they get to do more stuff and share the same experiences, while I'm still trying to catch up. 99
> *Girl, age 13*

The youngest child is often considered the "baby" of the family long after the actual baby years.

If you're seen as the "baby," everyone in the family may still treat you like a little kid. Your parents may not see that you're growing up, even if the evidence is right in front of their face.

On the flip side, being the "baby" may mean you get star treatment in your family—meaning everyone dotes on you and looks out for you. (Not such a bad deal.)

Either way, youngest children share something in common: their parents tend to be more relaxed and experienced by the time the "baby" comes along. Less worry from them means less pressure on you.

Youngest children are more likely to:

- ☑ Like being the center of attention
- ☑ Be the class clown
- ☑ Be outgoing, charming, and social
- ☑ Need to prove themselves
- ☑ Seek praise and encouragement
- ☑ Stick with something until they succeed
- ☑ Be affectionate

Whether you're the first, middle, or last child, you don't have to be a certain way. You're still your own person and can make choices about how you think and act.

If you see a little of yourself in the checklists you've just read through, and you like what you see, great! If you think you understand your siblings better now, that's great, too. If there are changes you want to make in yourself or in your relationships, that's what this book is for. Either way, keep reading. As you read, think about how your birth order and your sibs' birth order plays a role in how you get along.

Top 10 Sticky Situations and Survival Secrets for Sibs

Kids say they're sick of the:

Bickering!

Battling!

Teasing!

Tattling!

Competing!

Complaining!

Sneaking!

Peeking!

Hogging!

Bugging!

Lying!

Denying!

Bossing!

Spying!

Disagreeing!

Refereeing!

1. "No fair!"

(Your parents seem to take sides or play favorites.)

> ❝ How come my brother always gets away with stuff? I'm always the one to blame, even when *he* starts it. It just makes me get even madder at him. ❞
>
> *Boy, age 8*

Maybe you think your sister gets her way all the time or doesn't get punished as often as you do. Maybe she's older and seems to run the show, or maybe she's younger and "doesn't know any better," according to your parents. How unfair is that?

You've probably heard adults say,

"Life isn't fair."

And you probably thought,

"Sure, THAT helps."

No situation is ever 100 percent fair because it's just not possible—life is more complicated than dividing up a pie so everyone gets an equal piece. Even if things *were* totally equal, it may not feel good. Why? Because deep down every child in the family wants a little more than their share. Lots of kids secretly wish to be their parents' favorite, at least sometimes. This is normal.

No matter how hard your parents try to treat you and your sibs equally, you may not think it's enough. Do you spend a lot of time "keeping score" of who got more (or less)? If so, you're probably spending time you *could* be spending on chances to grow and have fun. That means you're not being fair to *yourself*.

Flex.

If your sibling seems to get more attention from Mom or Dad, stop and ask yourself why. Does your sib *need* more help or struggle more than you do? Be flexible (or willing to change)—and give people the benefit of the doubt. Flexibility is a skill that can help you at home, at school, and on the playing field. Stretch yourself even further by giving your sib chances to "win." You might let your sib have the bigger piece of pizza, sit in the best chair, or go first in a game. What's in it for you? You'll start to get along better, and that feels good.

P.S. If you take a hard look and can't see any reason for the way your parents treat you, talk to them about it. Use a calm voice, be honest, and suggest what you want to change.

ACTION PLAN

If you and your sibs argue a lot and it seems like you never get a fair deal, have a family member step in and act as a mediator. (*Mediate* means helping people who disagree come up with a solution that works for everyone.)

Here are four steps for the mediator to follow:

1. Listen to each side of the story and repeat aloud what you heard to make sure it's correct.

2. Ask each person involved for possible solutions to the problem. Write down each solution so everyone can see it.

3. Choose the two best solutions and ask each person to agree to try one of them. (If the people involved can't agree, the mediator picks the solution.) Have everyone shake hands to show they're ready to make peace.

4. Try the chosen solution to see if it works. If it doesn't, start the mediation process over again.

2. "Give it back!"

(You and your sibs fight about your stuff.)

Part of the fun of having siblings is sharing and borrowing each other's stuff—unless your sib has some bad habits:

- breaks things or doesn't put them back

- uses up your paper, shampoo, or other supplies (and doesn't bother telling you)

- reads your books and returns them with bent and sticky pages

- borrows your clothes and leaves them in a smelly heap

- loses your stuff and blames anybody else—you, another sib, the dog

- expects you to share but won't share in return

- never even bothers to ask!

Your belongings mean something to you—and they deserve to be treated with respect. (So do you.)

If your sib has any of the bad habits on page 29, speak up. Talk to your sib, and your mom or dad, too. A family meeting might help. See pages 65–67 for more about that.

If *you're* the one with the scary sharing habits, it's time to make a change. Treat your sibs' stuff the way you want *your* stuff treated, starting today.

Set an example.

Always ask permission to use your sib's things instead of helping yourself—then your sib is more likely to do the same. What if your brother or sister says "no" when you want to borrow something? Offer a trade: "I'll let you use my video game if I can use your skateboard." If the answer is still no, should you say, "Great, thanks a lot, butthead"? Well, maybe not. Instead, try saying, "Okay, thanks for considering it." By not arguing or complaining, you set an example and show that you're mature. Keep that up, and your sib may be more likely to say yes next time.

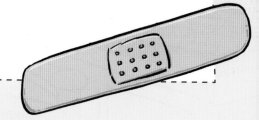

3. "Leave me alone!"

(There's not enough privacy.)

Are your siblings Space Invaders? (Always getting in your space and your face?)

Everyone needs privacy. It's normal to want to be on your own sometimes, whether you're in a good mood or a bad one. Being alone gives you time to chill, think, and dream. Maybe you need quiet time to get your homework done, practice your instrument, or spend time on a hobby. Then, just when you get a moment to yourself, in barges your sib, wanting attention.

> **My sister and I often argue with each other. But after we talked, I learned that she felt I was ignoring her and that acting up was the only way she felt she could get my attention. So now I play with her, even if it means playing dolls with her. I don't like it, but I see that she does—and now she doesn't bug me so much.**
>
> *Boy, age 13*

Quid pro quo.

(Quid-pro-huh?) *Quid pro quo* is a Latin expression meaning "Something for something." Basically, you *give* something to *get* something in return. Here's how it works: If your sib keeps asking you to play or won't stop bugging you, suggest a *qpq* agreement like, "I'll play one game with you if you agree to give me some alone time for 30 minutes." Shake on it, and then set a timer if needed.

Here's a set of privacy rules to try with your brothers and sisters. You and your sibs can make a privacy poster to hang up, if you'd like.

PRIVACY RULES

* Respect each other's "alone time." (Say "I need some alone time" so it's clear when you want to be on your own.)

* Respect each other's space. (Knock before entering. Enter only if invited.)

* Journals, text messages, and emails are PRIVATE.

* No spying.

* No bathroom-barging (the door is closed for a reason).

4. "Hey, what about me?!"

(Problems with the sib social scene.)

Part of the fun of having sibs is that you have other kids to hang with and play with whenever you want. This automatically increases your social life.

But what if your sibs are "fair-weather friends"? (They're friendly only when they're bored or need something from you.) Maybe they ditch you the moment a friend comes over. Or they make plans with you and break them the instant something "better" comes along. Maybe your sib's idea of spending time with you looks like this:

If you want your sibs to spend more time with you, one question to ask yourself is:

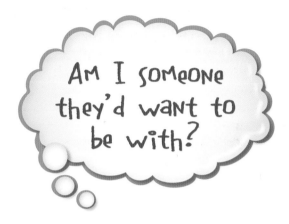

If you bug your sibs a lot, tease them, or tattle on them, it's going to be harder to get the positive attention you want. But it's not too late to change this. Being friends with your sibs means acting like a *friend*. Friends treat each other with respect.

Start small. Ask your brother to toss the football with you for 20 minutes. Paint your sister's toenails or take the dog for a walk together. The key is to find something you *both* like to do, do it for a short time so you don't get on each other's nerves, and then go your separate ways for a while. After hanging out together, say "That was fun" or "Thanks for spending time with me."

> **❝** My parents tell me I have to let my little sister play with us when my friends come over. But she starts whining if she doesn't like what we're doing, and my friends get tired of it and they go home! **❞**
>
> *Boy, age 8*

Sometimes, spending time with a sibling can feel like a chore, worse than doing a mountain of dishes or brushing the dog's teeth. This can be especially true if you have a friend over and Dad or Mom suggests you include your sib, too. If you get in this situation, you could agree to let your sister or brother join in for a specific amount of time (maybe a half hour). Choose an activity that's fun for three or more people to do. You might all end up having more fun than you expected, but if not—*ding!*—the time limit gives you an "out."

By the way, this also works if you're the sib who wants to be included—ask to join for a half hour or so, and be a good sport while you play (see pages 97–100 for more on that). You might even get invited to stay.

5. "It's MY turn!"

(Fights break out over who gets to use what.)

These days, many families have lots of cool things—especially electronics—and everyone wants to use them. Do you and your sibs have trouble sharing? Maybe you argue over who gets to use the phone first or which TV shows to watch. Maybe it seems like the older kids in the family get more screen time, or that whenever you want to use something, someone else got there first. What's a family to do?

Go outside.

Outdoors you can run, jump, yell, and hide—
and sharing doesn't seem like as big of a deal.
If the weather's lousy, you and your sib could
do something indoors that doesn't involve
sharing—draw, listen to music, play charades,
or get two decks of cards for a fun game of
double solitaire.

With a parent's help, set up
some guidelines at home.

- Make a schedule of family screen time
  (who can use what when).

- Use a timer to keep track of each person's time.

- Find ways to earn extra minutes, like helping out
  more at home.

- Do other things besides sitting in front of screens.
  Have a family board game night, play softball
  together, go to a park, dance, or do crafts.

6. "Make him stop!"

(There's too much teasing and fighting.)

Teasing happens in most families—and it's not all bad. Poking fun at someone in a funny, loving way is okay as long as you don't cross the line into meanness. Maybe you joke about how much time your brother spends in front of the mirror, or you like to retell the story of your sister's pants falling down when she was jumping on a trampoline. You can usually get away with this if you let your sibs tease you, too.

> I do tease my sisters—it's just part of life. I'll take their blanket, tap them on the shoulder, and say it wasn't me—it was a ghost named Bob.
>
> *Boy, age 9*

But sometimes siblings take teasing too far. Do you and your sibs call each other names? Put each other down? Make fun of each other's appearance or clothes?

> ❝I don't like it when my brother calls me 'Chubby Cheeks' in front of my friends. It's embarrassing.❞
> *Boy, age 10*

Living together means you know each other well—and you know just which buttons to push. You've seen your sibs' sensitive spots. You know what hurts. It's easy to use that knowledge against your sister or brother in the heat of the moment—but you probably don't feel good afterward.

Harsh teasing hurts, especially when it comes from someone in your family. Your home is supposed to be the one place in the world where you can be completely yourself. It's hard to relax if you know the teasing could start at any time.

Suppose your brother calls you a rude name—is your usual reaction to call him something worse? Then the two of you go at it until Mom or Dad shows up?

Next time teasing happens, you might say,

"Please stop teasing me. I don't like it."

Then . . .

Walk away.

Yes, it's hard to do, until you do it so often it's automatic. Ignore the mean name—and don't believe for a second that the criticism is true. Leave the room and go find something fun to do. Even if your brother or sister follows you around saying stupid stuff, pretend you don't care. When people are ignored over and over, they usually get the message.

Here's another idea to try. If you're getting teased, ask the teaser silly questions. Start each question with the words *who, what, when, where, why,* or *how* and use a calm tone. Like this:

"you're such a loser!"

Who told you that?

What do you mean?

When did I lose?

Where was I a loser?

Why do you care?

How do you know?

Why do you say that?

Each time the teaser responds, ask another question from the list. Don't tease back, because that just makes it worse. Keep calmly asking questions and eventually, the teaser will give up because you're not getting upset. Ask a parent or friend to "role play" this kind of conversation with you so you get the hang of it.

7. "How come *I* can't do that?"

(Your sibs seem to get more privileges.)

One of the hardest things about having older siblings is that they'll always be older and it seems like they'll always have more privileges. Your sister or brother may get more things, get to stay out later, or get to go more places alone. This may seem unfair, but someday you'll have those same privileges yourself. Sure, it's hard to wait—but your day will come.

Besides, your sib doesn't have it all easy. Being older usually means more responsibilities, harder homework, bigger chores, higher expectations from adults, and maybe an after-school job.

Ask for what you want.

Maybe your parents don't realize you're ready for more privileges and the responsibilities that come with them. It doesn't hurt to ask for what you need. Use a grown-up voice when you do, so you don't sound like you're whining or complaining. Here's one way of saying it: "Dad, can you explain why Derek gets to go outside with his friends more than I do? It feels unfair, but maybe there's a reason."

You'll be older soon enough, and if your behavior is good, you'll have a better chance of getting some of the same privileges that your sib has now. (You might even get them sooner if your parents think you're ready for them.) Ask your dad or mom if there's anything you can do—like improving your grades or doing more chores—to earn privileges sooner.

8. "She's better than me!"

(Jealousy and competition at home.)

Admit it: You get jealous of your brother or sister, don't you? That's totally normal. All siblings feel jealous at some point, even when they're grown up and supposed to be acting like adults. The truth is some sibs feel jealous nearly every day.

Maybe you're jealous when your brother gets higher grades or more awards than you do. Maybe you envy the way your sister makes friends easily and sweet-talks your parents into letting her have a second dessert. Maybe you think your parents play favorites.

Jealousy can sneak up on you anytime. You might even feel jealous of things that you know don't matter much (like your sister was the first one to the car and took the front seat). What's up with that?

The Jealousy Monster is on your back again!

This monster has a way of inviting himself in and sticking around. Then, each time you see your sib getting any praise or attention, it's like the monster is tapping you on the shoulder and saying, "Did you see that? Doesn't that make you *mad?!*" It may help to remember that you and your sib aren't in a competition—it's okay to stop acting like you are.

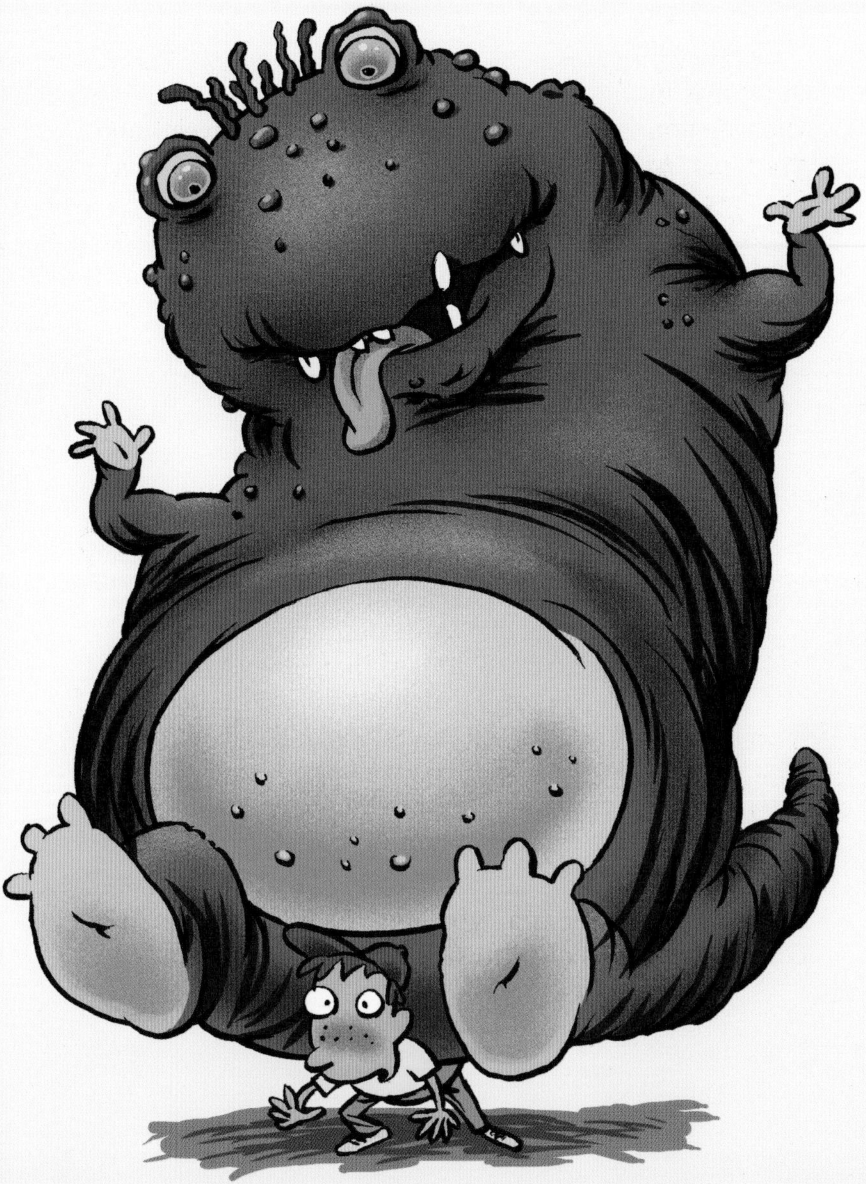

Take a time-out from competing.

It's natural for sibs to compete in all sorts of ways at home. Maybe you run races to see who's fastest, or you play competitive board games or video games. Maybe you have burping contests that gross out the whole family. Time to put a stop to that, at least for a while, so you can break the competition habit and get the Jealousy Monster off your back. You and your sib can do fun *non*competitive activities like making cookies or renting a movie you both like.

Of course, *some* competition *can* be healthy, because it encourages you to try your best.

Think about sisters Venus and Serena Williams who've been called the greatest sibling tandem in the history of professional sports (tandem, meaning partners). These two sisters have played tennis together since the age of five, and they've won championships across the world. Along the way, the two of them learned not to let their wins and losses get in the way of being close sisters. Venus, the older sister, once said, "I always like to win. But I'm the big sister. I want to make sure Serena has everything, even if I don't have anything." And her sister Serena has said, "Family's first, and that's what matters most. We realize that our love goes deeper than the tennis game."

The bonds with your sibs can be that strong, too.

> **❝**I do get a little jealous of my brother sometimes because I think he gets more time with our mom, and he's better at math. Also, he gets more presents.**❞**
>
> *Boy, age 8*

To get the Jealousy Monster off your back, try praising your siblings for the things they're good at. At first, it may feel weird to say "Way to go," or "I'm proud of you," but you'll get used to it. If you can't say it, give a high five or thumbs up. This feels better than being miserable and jealous! Pretty soon, your sibs will start praising you, too.

Some kids who have a sib with major talents or achievements decide to discover what they're good at, so they have their own place to shine. Find out what you love to do—then do it for the fun of it. With time and practice, your skills will improve.

9. "I have to do *everything!*"

(The chores don't seem equal.)

If you have younger siblings, it might seem like they have it easy and they get away with everything. Maybe they leave their toys all over the floor and don't have any chores that you've ever seen them do. Or, maybe you baby-sit your sibs when your parents are out or at work, and you can't seem to get any help. This can be a real source of frustration.

Having chores and responsibilities is an important part of growing up. You're learning, a little at a time, how to become an adult. It's not always fun to have grown-up responsibilities, but it can be nice to have the freedoms and privileges that go along with being older. Maybe the extra chores and baby-sitting are a way to earn money, which helps a little, too.

Sometimes, it may seem like you have a lot more chores than your sibs, when in fact you don't. Maybe your sibs have age-appropriate chores, meaning the tasks are simpler but right for a child's age. You might not be around when your sisters and brothers are doing their chores—or maybe they do them faster than you do. Take a closer look at what's really going on. Ask your dad or mom for their views on the matter.

Would a chore chart help? Have your family make one together—a great project for a family meeting. See pages 65–67 for more on meetings.

10. "You're not the boss of me!"

(Communication breakdown among sibs.)

Do you have a sib who acts like the boss? Always telling the rest of you what to do or what you did "wrong"? Maybe this sib says stuff like:

Get busy on that homework, Mister.

I'm telling 'cause you didn't do what Dad said!

Dude, SHUT UP.

I'm older, so you'd better do what I say.

We're going to watch MY show. Get over it!

Because I said so, that's why.

You are SO going to get it when Mom comes home!

Wash my toes!*

*Okay, hopefully not that one.

Remember reading earlier about how your birth order can affect how you see yourself in your family? (Go back to pages 14–23 if you need a refresher.) It's not unusual for oldest/older siblings to see themselves as having to "take charge." So if you're the youngest child or somewhere in the middle, you might feel like you have a big bad boss even if you're not old enough to have a job.

Let's face it: no one likes being told what to do. The important word here is *told*. As in,

"Do it. Now. Hurry up. Get busy. **I said NOW!**"

Anyone who hears this is likely to feel angry, sad, scared, frustrated, hurt, bullied, or annoyed.

Youngest sibs sometimes act bossy, too (not just oldest sibs).

Now, imagine being *asked:*

> would you please turn down the music? I'm trying to study, and it would really help me if it was quieter.

Manners can make all the difference!

Whether you're the oldest, middle, or youngest, you can start a new communication trend in your family. Instead of *ordering* a sib to do something, try *asking.*

Politely.

With a **smile.**

Sometimes, saying someone's name when you ask can help, too, like this:

> Hey, Maria, I was wondering, can we do the dishes together tonight? you wash, and I'll dry—or the other way around. Okay?

If your sister or brother starts up with the bossy remarks or demands, you could say:

> I'd be more willing to do it if you'd ask me **politely.**

> I think you forgot the magic word. It's **please.**

> I like it better when you talk to me **nicely.**

Use a calm voice and look your sib in the eye.

Your sib may not respond in the most mannerly way—at least not at first. But if you keep being polite in as many situations as you can at home, it's bound to rub off on your sib . . . eventually.

ACTION PLAN

There are a few important words that families often forget when life gets busy. But using these words makes communication so much easier (and more polite). Try them every day:

SAY WHAT?	WHEN?
Please	When you want something
Thank you	When someone gives you what you want or does what you ask
You're welcome	When someone says "Thank you"
Excuse Me	Whenever you bump into someone, need to get by people, or have to interrupt someone who's talking
Yes, please	When you want something being offered to you
No, thank you	When you don't want what's being offered
I'm sorry	When you hurt someone or make a mistake

5 Ways to Forge a Fabulous Friendship

1. Meet, greet, take a seat

Do you want a stronger family?
Better relationships with your sibs?
A fresh way to let your voice be heard?

Family meetings are your chance to sit down with your family face-to-face and work together. Ask your family if you can meet for at least 15 minutes once a week to (drum roll, please) COMMUNICATE.

In a family meeting, each person gets a chance to share opinions and feelings. Talk to your dad or mom about it first, and then use the tips in this section.

Set some ground rules.

Make full-participation a must—everyone shows up, everyone has a say. Turn off any electronics (the TV, hand-held video games, cell phones) that might distract you. Hold the meeting in the same place each time, with everyone seated. No teasing or name-calling in meetings.

Make an agenda.

Meetings can be a time to talk about sibling conflicts and solve problems. Write down the issues each person wants to bring up. Make sure people speak calmly—no yelling or whining. Ask for a parent's help in working things out.

Get a good vibe going.

Start the meeting on a positive note by giving each person a compliment, telling jokes, or thanking someone for a favor. How about some tasty treats?

Let everyone be heard.

Take turns talking without interrupting each other. You may even want to pass around an object that the speaker holds each time. For example, you could have a "talking stick," a microphone with the sound turned off, or a lightsaber (keep that turned off, too). Some families make a special hat for the speaker to wear. If you'd like, let the youngest child talk first—or take turns going first each week.

Set a timer.

Usually, 15 minutes is a good time-frame for a family meeting, but you may need more. Whatever length of time you agree to, when the timer goes off, you are done.

End on a high note.

Play a quick game, read an inspiring quote, or join hands and say one thing you're grateful for—whatever helps you feel connected.

Make sure "Family Meeting" gets put on the calendar each week—same time, same place—so everyone is on board.

2. Check your feet

Go find a pair of your sister's or brother's shoes. (Be sure to get permission first. And hey, sorry if they stink!)

Now try on the shoes. How do they feel? Big, small, tight, roomy, pinchy, comfy?

Walk around in them a while, thinking about that old saying "Take a walk in someone else's shoes." It means to put yourself in the other person's place—imagining life from his or her view.

You're wearing your sib's shoes . . . now think about how certain situations might look and feel to your brother or sister.

Does the amount of chores at our house seem fair—why or why not?

How does the family treat me?

Who has more privileges and responsibilities at home? Why?

When I get teased, I feel _____ .

What makes me angry, sad, jealous?

I wish _____ would change at home.

I'm trying hard to get along when I do this: _____ .

I know my brother/sister loves me because

_____ .

This exercise can help you see your sibs in a new light. After walking in their shoes, ask yourself:

"Is there something I'm doing to make things worse for my sib?"

"Is there something I can do to make things better?"

3. If you can't stand the heat...

Have you ever heard the phrase, "If you can't stand the heat, get out of the kitchen"? It means if you don't like the way something is, then get away from it.

Leave.

Skeedaddle.

Bonding with sibs isn't always easy. You may still have nit-picky fights—hey, stop *touching* me!—and days that go from bad to worse. That's okay. Take a breather when you need one. Time away from each other can help you relax and think about what's going on.

Think of it as pushing your reset button.

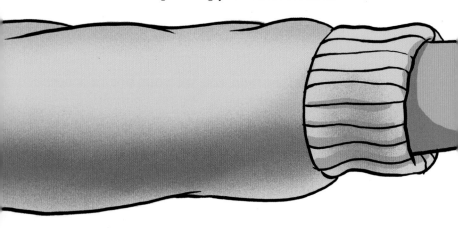

Here are some ways to **chill out:**

- Move your body (ride your bike, take a walk, dance, run, swing, swim, practice karate, jump rope).

- Work on your hobby or do some crafts.

- Write in a journal.

- Sketch, paint, or draw funny cartoons.

- Make music or listen to your favorite tunes.

- Grab a hunk of clay: pound it out, shape it, sculpt it.

RESET BUTTON

★ Dig around in a garden or sandbox. (Ask if it's okay.)

★ Find a quiet place where you can go to feel peaceful (under a tree, in your closet, on a park bench).

★ Talk to someone you trust about your feelings.

★ Spend time enjoying nature.

★ Read a book or magazine.

★ Love your pet.

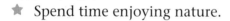

★ Write letters or emails to people you care about.

★ Volunteer—helping someone else is a great way to feel good about yourself and the world.

★ Do some deep breathing to relax. Start by breathing in and imagining your breath is a wave: it comes in through your toes and washes up through your body and all the way to the top of your head. Count to five slowly as you do this. Then breathe out, counting backward from five, slowly. Picture the wave washing back down through your body, down to your toes, and out to sea. Continue breathing like this for a few minutes, or as long as you like. You'll know you're taking deep breaths if your belly rises and falls as you breathe in and out.

4. Be sweet

If you want to get along better with a sib, try this experiment. For one week, do your best to be as nice as you can be to your brother or sister, even if he or she isn't being so nice to you.

Here are some examples:

- Say "Hi," "Good morning," and "Goodnight."

- Ask your sib, "How's it going?" or "What's up?"

- Offer to help with homework or chores.

- Give at least one compliment a day: "Cool hair, dude."

- When you say good-bye, add something like, "Have a good day!"

- If you notice that your sib is in a bad mood, instead of calling him or her Crankenstein, ask, "Is everything okay? Anything I can do to help?"

- Be encouraging: "Way to go," "Nice job," "Good try!"

During the week, try not to criticize, tease, or fight. At the end of the week, think about how the experiment went. Did you notice a positive difference? If the answer is yes, then you've discovered the secret to getting along!

5. Rinse. Repeat.*

You've been reading about lots of ways to get along with sibs and make your relationship stronger. You've also learned tips for improving family communication. And ***presto-chango!*** Now your family is perfect, and you and your sibs never, ever fight—right?

Okay, probably not.

*The instructions on shampoo bottles used to always recommend "Wash. Rinse. Repeat." Why? Maybe the Shampoo Geniuses thought everyone had really dirty hair—or maybe they just wanted to sell more shampoo. Whether you wash your hair twice or not, we'd like you to think about the idea of "Repeat." As in: "Do it again." Sometimes even: "Again and again." Repeating a positive action can be helpful because it's a form of *practice*. Practice leads to success.

Making changes takes time and repeated effort. Don't give something one try only and expect it to work just the way you wanted. One family meeting, for example, won't be enough. And you'll need to take a walk in your sib's shoes (looking at something from his or her point of view) more than once, too. The experiment about "being sweet" to your sib lasts for a week—but you can repeat it as often as needed, until being kind becomes a habit at home.

Keep trying and don't give up. Whenever you need encouragement, talk to a parent or another adult you trust.

Stick Together!
(Bonding as Sibs)

> **❝** The best things about having an older brother are that he keeps me company, he plays with me, and since he's one grade ahead, he tells me which teachers are nice and what to expect. **❞**
>
> *Girl, age 9*

> **❝** One nice thing about having a sister is that I always have someone at home to play with. **❞**
>
> *Boy, age 11*

> **“** I love my brother. Life wouldn't be the same without him around. He's funny and weird and wild, and we laugh all the time because of him. **”**
>
> *Girl, age 10*

> **“** My sisters are in high school, and I'm still in middle school. They give me the 411 on which teachers are good, so I'm less nervous about going to high school. **”**
>
> *Girl, age 13*

Build a better bond

One key to building a strong sibling relationship is spending time with each other. That sounds easy enough, right? (Sometimes it probably seems like you can never get away from each other.) But if you and your sibs mostly spend your time together watching TV or hitting each other in the backseat while Dad runs errands, that doesn't build a bond. Try spending some **Quality Time (QT)** together instead.

What is quality time? Time spent having fun, getting to know each other better, helping each other, laughing, and feeling like friends but even closer. Having more shared experiences and shared projects is a great way to connect.

Shared experiences:

- Cook dinner together for the family, invent new recipes, create make-your-own sundaes or build-your-own mini pizzas.

- Talk about things you don't ordinarily talk about: What were your dreams last night? If you could be any book character, who would it be and why? If you were a superhero, what powers would you most want to have? What is the weirdest thing that ever happened to you?

- Go to fun places with your family: mini-golf, a water park, a museum, a free concert, a local park or wildlife center—anything that gets you out of your home and lets you explore.

- Co-host an outdoor event for your family and friends: a softball or kickball game, a picnic, a water balloon fight, a badminton tournament, an obstacle course, or wacky races.

- Have fun doing karaoke, dance contests, or the limbo.

Even just 15 minutes of QT a day can make a difference in your relationship.

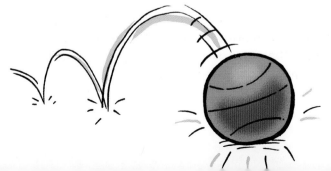

Stick together tip:

Say I ♥ U.

Is your family big on spreading the love, often saying "I love you" and giving hugs and kisses? For some families, those three little words can be hard to say—and the affection may be forgotten when life is busy. You and your sibs can show you care for each other by hugging once in a while, signing emails with "Love ya," or giving high fives or fist bumps.

Shared projects:

- If you share a bedroom, talk to your parents about you and your sib having the chance to figure out how the space will be used, how to organize and decorate, and how to create private areas within a common space. Working together on a big project like this helps you get to know each other better, plan, dream, and create something lasting.

- Build something together—anything! A Lego city, a backyard clubhouse, a clay volcano that erupts, a birdhouse, a fort, or giant sandcastles.

- Make up a scavenger hunt. Create a list of weird, wild, or gross things you can find outside, make copies of the list for each sibling, and head out. Here are some ideas to get you started on your list: an ice-cream stick, a piece of bark, a rock with two colors (or a smooth rock, or a jagged rock), a dandelion, a piece of litter (or two, or five), a dead leaf, a dead bug, a live bug, an abandoned mitten, a nail or screw, a ball. Or bring digital cameras (or cell phones) and take pictures of the items on your list—then you can add things it would be impossible to carry, like a bird in a tree or a white fence.

- Be entrepreneurs together by setting up a lemonade stand, making bracelets to sell, baby-sitting, pet sitting, dog walking, doing yard work for neighbors, or producing a 'zine to sell to friends and family. Make a flyer to advertise your services. The money you earn can go toward something you want to buy together—maybe concert tickets or a video game console. Or, you might decide to donate your earnings to a worthy cause you and your sib support.

- Write plays or musicals together, create costumes, build the sets or make scenery, and have fun performing. Invite the neighbors for your big production or set up a video camera to record it on film.

Stick together tip:

Celebrate your family.

You and your sibs can write a funny poem about your family, make up a family cheer, create a secret handshake, or come up with a family motto. (A motto is a sentence or phrase that sums up your purpose.) You might also collect some family trivia to quiz each other or ask each other questions like "What's your earliest memory?" "If you could eat dinner with a famous person, dead or alive, who would it be and why?" Activities like these show you how unique your family is and can help you get closer.

How to bond with younger sibs

Being an older sibling has benefits. You probably get more privileges, like a later bedtime and extra spinach with dinner (your favorite!), and you have younger kids in the family looking up to you. You also get to teach your sibs things you already know, which gives you a chance to show your stuff. Here are some ideas for being a great older sister or brother:

1. **Praise and encourage younger sibs.** Say "Great job" when you see them trying hard. They'll feel good when you do, and they'll probably look for other ways to impress you. You'll be teaching your sibs positive ways to get your attention, which means they're less likely to bug or bother you at other times.

2. **Practice asking, not bossing.** It may be your role at home to help out your dad or mom by taking care of younger sibs. This may mean getting the other kids to do their chores, eat healthy foods, or finish their homework. If you have to take charge or be a leader, remember to be polite. Ask them nicely to do as you say. For example, "Jada, can you please help me pick up these toys?" If your sib does what you asked, smile and say thanks.

3. **Give them your time.** Younger sibs often want to spend time with older sibs, playing, talking, and watching (then copying) what they do. Sometimes, this tag-along stuff may bother you— but doesn't it also feel good knowing someone thinks you're cool just because you're older? Let your younger sibs watch you shoot hoops, "help" you with homework, or follow you around while you do chores. It can be fun to have someone keeping you company.

Stick together tip:

Support your sib.

Go to your sister's games, your brother's recitals, or any school events that each of you participate in. Cheer, clap, whistle, and holler to show your support. Be encouraging at home by talking to your sisters and brothers and asking them about their day. As an older sib, you have the chance to be a good listener and a Giver of Wise Advice.

4. **Do what they like to do.** So, your sister likes to play "house" all the time, your brother can't stop talking about his toy robot—and you're bored to tears. Try to put aside those feelings and join in sometimes, even if the activity sounds dull or too young for you. Your sibs will probably love having your attention, and you can even use it as a *reward*: "I'll play with you a while because you helped me clear the table."

5. **Let them make mistakes.** It's great to teach younger siblings a new skill, but remember they'll be looking to you for motivation. It may take many tries, and many mistakes, before your sibs succeed. Be patient. Stay encouraging. Let them keep trying. That's how they learn and grow.

In the game of golf, players are sometimes given a "handicap," or an adjustment to their score if people are at different ability levels. This way, all players have an equal chance of winning. What does this have to do with being an older sib? Plenty!

You might be better at games and sports than your younger sister or brother—but you still want to play together and have fun. Sometimes, you can give your sib a handicap so things are more even. For example:

- When it's to your sib's advantage, make the rule "Youngest goes first."

- If you're playing a board game, let your sib move his or her game piece a few spots ahead of yours before you start.

- During sports, play with your opposite hand or give your sib pointers for improving his or her performance.

- Don't enforce the game rules too strictly, especially if your little brother or sister is showing signs of frustration. After all, if you *always* win and your sib *always* loses, what fun is that?

✖✖✖✖✖✖✖✖✖✖✖✖✖✖✖✖✖✖✖✖✖✖✖✖✖✖✖✖✖✖✖

Question: When you beat your younger sibling in a game, it's always nice to:

A. Say, "You suck!"

B. Jump up on the table, dance the funky chicken, and sing "I am the champion!"

C. Compliment your sibling on a good game and offer to help him or her learn to improve.

Answer: C, for *see* how nice you are?

How to bond with older sibs

Younger sibs often feel left out or left behind. Maybe you want to spend time with your older sibs, but it seems like they're always busy or they think you're kind of a pain. They might even say you're "spoiled" compared to them or that you don't do your fair share at home. If you want to be seen as a super younger sib, try these ideas:

1. **Respect their privacy.** Don't bother your older siblings if they want to be left alone. (Teens need more privacy than younger kids and may feel like you're bugging them if you don't respect that.) Be sure not to go in your brother's or sister's room without knocking or asking first. (Check out the privacy rules on page 35.)

2. **Respect their quiet time.** Older kids usually need extra time to do their homework because they have a lot more of it. Try not to interrupt your sibs when they're busy with homework, practicing an instrument, or working on something that requires concentration.

3. **Ask nicely—no whining.** If you want your older sibs to play with you or hang out, ask *politely* for 20 minutes of their time. Avoid saying "Play with me! Play with me! Mom said!" Instead try, "Will you please play a few games of checkers with me? For maybe 20 minutes?" Be a good sport, too (see pages 97–100 for more on that).

4. **Show your appreciation.** If an older brother or sister helps you out or does a favor for you, remember to say "thank you." Your sib will feel good when you show your appreciation. You could make your sister or brother a card as a special way of saying thanks.

5. **Try not to depend too much on older sibs.** Part of growing up is making friends and learning to find your own way in life. If you have friends your own age at school or in the neighborhood, you won't feel as lonely when your sibs are busy or they need time alone. It's also important to enjoy your own company—so spend time each day relaxing by yourself, doing quiet activities, or playing alone.

6. **Get advice.** If you feel left out at home, talk to your dad, your mom, or another trusted adult. You might say, "I feel lonely sometimes" or "I want more attention from my sister/brother—what can I do?"

Stick together tip:

Get camera-happy.

Take funny photos of you and your sibs doing all those silly things sibs do (like dressing up in weird outfits for Guitar Hero, making funny faces, capturing your sib's bed-head on camera, or attacking each other with the garden hose). Have your dad or mom take pictures when you and your sibs are having fun and getting along so you have a record of those important moments.

Spend time as a family putting the photos in scrapbooks or on computer slide shows. It's fun to print doubles of your photos so you can use the extras for display around your home. Hang them on the fridge or, if you're "crafty," make decorative frames or cut out the heads/bodies on the photos for mix-and-match collage creations.

Be a good sport

Have you ever noticed what sometimes happens when brothers and sisters get together to play a game? The screaming, the yelling, the—OUCH!—hitting. Sometimes, the rules of good sportsmanship seem to fly right out the window.

If playing with your siblings leads to arguments and hurt feelings, it may help to post a reminder about being a good sport.

Here are 10 tips for your family to follow:

Remember

Be a GOOD SPORT!!

1. Pick a game that everyone has a fair chance of winning. If the game requires more skill than one of your sibs has, then choose a different game.

2. If you can't agree on a game, take turns playing one you like and one your sib likes. (Flip a coin to see who picks first.)

3. Take turns going first, especially with activities that include longer turns (like video games). If you went first last time you played, give your sib the chance to go first this time.

4. Root for the other player. If your sister makes a good move, let her know! If she makes a not-so-good move, don't rub it in her face. You could say, "Nice try" or "No way, you got robbed." Being encouraging makes it more fun to play together.

5. If your sib seems to be getting frustrated with the game, step in and help. (You might first ask, "Hey, want some help?") Sometimes, giving a little advice or a few hints keeps the game going.

6. If you win the game, don't brag about it or tease your sib for losing. Don't parade around the room, saying "In your face!" Just say something like "Good game—maybe you'll win next time."

7. If you lose the game, congratulate your sister or brother on winning. Saying "Way to go!" or "You played really well" shows your sib there are no hard feelings.

8. If you're playing an athletic game, shake hands or give high fives after it's over to show good sportsmanship.

9. Don't cheat. Cheating isn't fair—plus, it just isn't cool. No one wants to play with someone who doesn't play by the rules.

10. Remember, the reason people play games is to have *fun*. So, have fun! Who cares if you win or lose? Do your best, learn from your mistakes, and know that in most games *luck* plays a part in how things turn out. If you don't win, better luck next time.

Stick together tip:

Party hearty.

Pick a weekend night for a sibs-only slumber party at home. Get out the sleeping bags, bunk together in the same bed, or make a fort out of a table covered with blankets. If you have a tent, maybe you could sleep in the backyard (ask your parents first). Plan a menu of your favorite foods and make them together. Choose activities that help you bond: tell ghost stories, consult the Magic 8-Ball, practice dance moves, watch home videos, and play outdoor or indoor games you love.

What if you're a "blended" family?

Millions of kids live in families in which their parents have divorced. Many of these parents find new partners and may remarry or move in with each other. This can be great if you like your new stepparent. But getting along with a stepparent's kids can be another challenge.

Maybe you were used to being the oldest in a family, with all the privileges that come with that. Suddenly an older stepsibling moves in and you're no longer "on top." Or, if you're the youngest and like the attention you get, a new stepsibling might seem to be taking that away from you. What if your parent and his or her new partner have a new baby together? That may be tough, at least at first.

Of course, good things come with blended families, too! You might get a stepsib who's close to your own age, which means you could have the same interests and activities. You may get the older brother you always wanted, or the younger sister you wished you had. You might even end up becoming best friends with your stepsibs. And if a new baby is on the way, you might be excited about helping out.

Remember, how you deal with your family situation is up to you. Here are some ideas to help you get along with new siblings.

- Give them a chance. After all, they may be feeling much like you do. It takes time to get to know each other and figure out how to get along.

- Ask them what they like to do for fun. See if you enjoy the same activities or if your stepsibs can teach you something new.

- Ask their advice on what to do about a problem. That can make them feel closer to you and helps you get to know each other better.

- If your new sibs now go to your school, offer to show them around and introduce them to some of your friends.

- Give your stepsibs a chance to get to know your mom or dad. It can be hard for them to get used to a new parent, especially if you're acting jealous or showing a lot of frustration.

- Offer to help with the new baby. This gives you a chance to bond with the baby and show your stepparent that you're trying to accept the way your family has changed.

If problems come up, complaining will not help—instead, try working things out. Use the ideas throughout this book and see if things improve. Talk to your parents about what's going on. Ask for support. And if one of your new siblings is making life very difficult for you or possibly hurting you in some way, tell an adult you trust. You need to feel safe.

What if your sib has special needs?

Some brothers or sisters have special problems (sometimes called "disorders") that can make life more difficult for them—and for you. Maybe your sib has a physical disability, has trouble learning or paying attention, is overly active, gets angry often, feels sad much of the time, or isn't very social with family members or other people. This isn't easy for anyone in the family. Your sib struggles, your mom or dad has more challenges than most parents, and you—as the brother or sister of someone with special needs—get caught up in it all.

Family life in these situations tends to be stressful at times. Your sib might not be able to play with you well, do many chores, handle strong emotions, or participate in a "normal" way. Families end up adjusting to a different kind of "normal"—but that can actually turn out to be a good thing. Sometimes, having a family member with special needs helps everyone in the family grow even closer because of the daily challenges you share.

No matter how much you love your sib, there will be times when you feel jealous, frustrated, embarrassed, or ignored. You may get angry when you see your sib getting extra attention from a parent, or when you see other people's reactions to your sib's behavior. At times, you might have to act as your sib's caregiver—and that's a lot of extra responsibility. You have more to handle than many kids your age. But with help from your family, teachers, or a counselor who can talk to you about your feelings, you'll have the support you need to stay strong.

Having a sib who's special teaches you a lot about life at an early age. You're probably more mature than your peers. You might be more sensitive and understanding than other kids you know. You're seeing firsthand that being "different" brings you in touch with a community of families who are also different. Different doesn't mean "worse." Sometimes, what makes people different is also what makes them uniquely creative, gentle, funny, intense, honest, or wise. Their differences help bring out their personal strengths.

For more info, check out page 115 for books on the ups and downs of life with a special sibling and about siblings getting along.

One more thing...

Reading this book is a start to being a better brother or sister. You've learned a lot already—but here's one more quiz to complete:

Your relationship with your sibs can . . . ?

A. Be a great chance to practice lots of creative insults

B. Help you learn to get along with people in life

C. Be as wild as wrestling greased alligators

D. Be as fun as a field trip to an all-you-can-eat pizza place

E. Last a lifetime

F. All of the above

Answer: It's F, of course—as in *eff*ort. What you get out of it depends on what you put into it.

A Note for Parents and Caregivers

Conflict between siblings is one of the most common parental complaints. You may wonder what you're doing wrong and if they'll ever outgrow it. It may seem like no matter what you do, someone ends up feeling upset or unloved. While kids say they want to be treated the same as their siblings, secretly, each child often wishes to be your favorite.

All siblings fight—it's perfectly normal. They disagree on what is fair, they compete, and they tease each other. Your job as a parent is to let kids work it out as much as possible, offer suggestions for solving problems when needed, and praise your kids when they resolve the conflict themselves.

Of course, being a good role model also is important. Kids learn by watching how you handle conflict and anger. Model and teach compassion if you want your children to show compassion to each other.

Other tips:

- Try to stop fights before they begin. Before dinner, for example, is a common time for sibling fights. If you can separate kids when they are angry, hungry, or tired, you will prevent many fights. Setting a schedule for items that need to be shared, such as TVs, computers, and video games will help.

- Give each child some time alone with you and with his or her friends. Too much together time can be hard on siblings. Don't expect them to interact cooperatively for hours at a time. If you give them more attention *after* the fighting starts, even if it's negative attention, you might be rewarding their bad behavior. Praise them for getting along well.

- Avoid labeling children. Referring to one child as the "good one" or "the apple of my eye" and another as the "bad one" or the "thorn in my side" not only can cause more competition and conflict between siblings but can damage their self-esteem.

When conflict erupts

As much as possible, watch from a distance when siblings squabble. It's hard, especially if you think one child is taking advantage of another. But if you intervene too quickly, you suggest to kids that they cannot solve their own problems and that they should rely on you to solve them. They may never learn to resolve conflict themselves.

If your children are unable to resolve an argument productively, or you sense that one child is becoming overwhelmed or about to lose his or her temper, then you can intervene. But your role should be that of a coach, not a "fixer." Listen to both sides and ask them to come up with solutions. If they are stuck, offer a few. Praise them for using constructive ways to solve the problem on their own.

When professional help is needed

Most sibling conflict is normal and will work itself out with time. If your children play well together at least some of the time, they will probably be okay. If one child bullies the others, fighting happens often and ruins family activities, or if a child's self-esteem suffers, consider counseling. Ask your child's teacher, guidance counselor, or healthcare provider for names of counselors in your area who work with kids. Family therapy can be an excellent way for kids (and parents) to learn new coping skills.

Resources for parents and caregivers

Beyond Sibling Rivalry: How to Help Your Children Become Cooperative, Caring, and Compassionate by Peter Goldenthal, Ph.D. Holt Paperbacks, 2000. Provides practical guidelines and tools for solving common and not-so-common sibling conflicts.

The Everything Parent's Guide to Raising Siblings: Tips to Eliminate Rivalry, Avoid Favoritism, and Keep the Peace by Linda Sonna, Ph.D. Adams Media, 2006. Learn how sibling relationships develop over time and how to resolve issues that provoke conflict. Contains practical advice for bringing up trustworthy, dependable, cooperative children who view their siblings as equals.

Loving Each One Best: A Caring and Practical Approach to Raising Siblings by Nancy Samalin. Bantam, 1997. Contains practical strategies for parents raising siblings, including topics such as adjustment to new siblings, parental fairness, sibling bickering, and dealing with children's differences.

Sibling Rivalry, Sibling Love: How to Ease Tension, Conflict and Develop Healthy, Happier Relationships by Jan Parker and Jan Stimpson. Hodder and Stoughton, Ltd., 2002. Helps parents manage siblings' difficult relationships, reduce conflict and frustration, and help children attain more positive fulfilling relationships.

Siblings Without Rivalry: How to Help Your Children Live Together So You Can Live Too by Adele Faber and Elaine Mazlish. Collins Living, 2004. Outlines ways to defuse such explosive situations as comparing, assigning roles, or taking sides and suggests specific remedies to avoid conflict.

Understanding Sibling Rivalry: The Brazelton Way by T. Berry Brazelton, M.D., and Joshua D. Sparrow, M.D. Da Capo Press, 2005. Shows how parents can defuse much of children's bickering, while helping to strengthen warm sibling relationships.

Books for kids who have sibs with special needs

All About My Brother by Sarah Peralta. Autism Asperger Publishing Company, 2002. An eight-year-old girl learns how to help and support her autistic younger brother.

Autism and Me: Sibling Stories by Ouisie Shapiro. Albert Whitman & Company, 2009. Kids tell what it's like to live with a sibling who has autism.

My Brother's a World Class Pain: A Sibling's Guide to ADHD/ Hyperactivity by Michael Gordon, Ph.D. G S I Publications, 1992. Explains what to expect if you have siblings with ADHD and how you can help them do their best.

The Sibling Slam Book: What It's Really Like to Have a Brother or Sister with Special Needs edited by Don Meyer. Woodbine House, 2005. More than 80 siblings talk about what it's really like to have a brother or sister with special needs. Read about their optimism, dedication, resentment, fierce protection, and love.

Views from Our Shoes: Growing Up with a Brother or Sister with Special Needs edited by Donald Meyer. Woodbine House, 1997. Forty-five kids ages 4 to 18 who have a sibling with special needs talk about their feelings. They admit to embarrassment, anger, and jealousy, but also show how protective, loving, and wise they are when it comes to getting along in a family that is different.

Your Seatbelt: A Crash Course on Down Syndrome and Siblings by Brian Skotko and Susan P. Levine. Woodbine House, 2009. Provides 100 questions and answers about the challenges of growing up with a sibling who has Down syndrome.

Index

About the Authors

James J. Crist, Ph.D. is a psychologist specializing in children with ADHD, depression, and anxiety disorders. He is the clinical director and a staff psychologist at the Child and Family Counseling Center in Woodbridge, Virginia, where he provides psychological testing and individual, couples, and family psychotherapy for children, adolescents, and adults.

Elizabeth Verdick is a children's book writer and editor. She lives in Minnesota with her husband and their two children.

Free Spirit's
Laugh & Learn® Series

Solid information, a kid-centric point of view, and a sense of humor combine to make each book in our Laugh & Learn series an invaluable tool for getting through life's rough spots. For ages 8–13. *Paperback; 80–136 pp.; illust.; 5⅛" x 7"*

Other Great Books from Free Spirit

Speak Up and Get Along!
by Scott Cooper

A handy toolbox of ways to get along with others, this book presents 21 strategies kids can learn and use to express themselves, build relationships, end arguments and fights, halt bullying, and beat unhappy feelings. Includes a note to adults. For ages 8–12.
Paperback; 128 pp.; two-color; illust.; 6" x 9"

The Survival Guide for Making and Being Friends
by James J. Crist, Ph.D.

Every kid's must-have primer for handling the ups, downs, ins, and outs of friendship. For ages 8–13.
Paperback; 128 pp.; two-color; illust.; 6" x 9"

Stick Up for Yourself!
by Gershen Kaufman, Ph.D., Lev Raphael, Ph.D., and Pamela Espeland

Simple words and real-life examples teach assertiveness, responsibility, relationship skills, choice making, problem solving, goal setting, anger management, and more. For ages 8–12.
Paperback; 128 pp.; illust.; 6" x 9"

Fighting Invisible Tigers
(Revised & Updated Third Edition)
by Earl Hipp

This book offers proven techniques that teens can use to deal with stressful situations in school, at home, and among friends. A great resource for any teen who's said, "I'm stressed out!" For ages 11 & up.
Paperback; 144 pp.; two-color; illust.; 6" x 9"

Interested in purchasing multiple quantities and receiving volume discounts?
Contact edsales@freespirit.com or call 1.800.735.7323 and ask for Education Sales.

Many Free Spirit authors are available for speaking engagements, workshops, and keynotes. Contact speakers@freespirit.com or call 1.800.735.7323.

For pricing information, to place an order, or to request a free catalog, contact:

Free Spirit Publishing Inc.
6325 Sandburg Road • Suite 100 • Minneapolis, MN 55427-3674
toll-free 800.735.7323 • local 612.338.2068 • fax 612.337.5050
help4kids@freespirit.com • www.freespirit.com